Teaching With Favorite Kevin Henkes Books

BY IMMACULA A. RHODES

SCHOLASTIC
PROFESSIONAL BOOKS

NEW YORK • TORONTO • LONDON • AUCKLAND • SYDNEY
MEXICO CITY • NEW DELHI • HONG KONG • BUENOS AIRES

For Alan and Amber,

my joy and inspiration...

"Be strong in the Lord and in his mighty power."

(Ephesians 6:10)

Cover illustration from WEMBERLY WORRIED by Kevin Henkes. Used by permission of HarperCollins Publishers. Copyright © 2000 by Kevin Henkes.

Cover illustration from LILLY'S PURPLE PLASTIC PURSE by Kevin Henkes. Used by permission of HarperCollins Publishers. Copyright © 1996 by Kevin Henkes.

Cover illustration from CHRYSANTHEMUM by Kevin Henkes. Used by permission of HarperCollins Publishers. Copyright © 1991 by Kevin Henkes.

Profile of Kevin Henkes from *The Big Book of Picture-Book Authors & Illustrators*, by James Preller (Scholastic Professional Books, 2001). Reprinted by permission of James Preller.

Photo of Kevin Henkes courtesy of Tom Beckley/HarperCollins.

Front cover and interior design by Kathy Massaro
Interior illustrations by Maxie Chambliss, except page 26 by Kate Flanagan, and page 42 by Shelley Dieterichs

ISBN 0-439-26080-9
Copyright © 2002 by Immacula A. Rhodes
Published by Scholastic Inc.
All rights reserved.
Printed in the U.S.A.

1 2 3 4 5 6 7 8 9 10   40   09 08 07 06 05 04 03 02

Contents

About This Book

Since 1981, Kevin Henkes has touched the hearts and lives of numerous children with his skillfully written and illustrated books. His lovable characters experience and respond to real-life conflicts and emotions in true childlike fashion. His art accurately captures the essence of their personalities and feelings. And his humor delights audiences of all ages. To introduce students to this award-winning author-illustrator, explore Kevin Henkes's stories and characters with the creative curriculum-related ideas in this author study.

This book offers an array of activities designed to help children explore and extend the books of Kevin Henkes. In these pages, you will find fresh, creative ideas to reinforce students' learning across the curriculum. Not only do the activities strengthen skills in literacy, math, science, and social studies, but they also promote emotional growth and help build positive character traits in children.

Here is an overview of what you'll find in this book:

◎ **Getting Started:** Choose from a collection of ideas to plan and prepare for your author theme. (See page 6.) Help children get to know Kevin Henkes with an insightful interview.

◎ **Teaching Activities for Any Time:** This section includes a wide range of ideas and reproducible activity pages for learning about different story elements, such as character, plot, setting, problem, and solution. It also features activities for exploring everyday emotions and behaviors. (See page 8.)

◎ **Lessons for Individual Books:** Beginning on page 18, you'll find complete lessons for eight books by Kevin Henkes, with activities and reproducible activity pages uniquely related to each title.

◎ **Activities for Teaching With More Books by Kevin Henkes:** Learn more with mini-lessons for three additional Keven Henkes books. Summaries and suggestions for using even more Kevin Henkes books let you take your author study further. (See pages 60–63.)

◎ **Author Study Celebration:** Wrap up your author study with activities that let children revisit the characters and events of Kevin Henkes's stories and celebrate what they've learned. (See page 64.)

Getting Started

From deciding how to plan your time, to setting up an area to display student work, here are some tips for planning a successful author study.

1. Decide how much time you plan to spend on your author study. Will you block off several weeks? Or will you study individual books in weekly intervals, spreading your study out over several months?

2. Gather and read the books that you plan to use in your study. Become familiar with the personalities, relationships, and conflicts of his characters. Note that some characters have recurring roles in several books.

3. Collect multiple copies of as many titles as possible.

4. Have volunteers record a selection of Kevin Henkes books on tape. (Or locate commercially prepared tapes.) Place the recordings in a listening center along with copies of the corresponding books.

5. Prepare a bulletin board and a table to display student work, book jackets, and a photo of Kevin Henkes.

Correlations to the Language Arts Standards

The activities in this book are designed to support you in meeting the following standards outlined by the Mid-Continent Regional Educational Laboratory (MCREL), an organization that collects and synthesizes national and state K–12 curriculum standards.

Uses the general skills and strategies of the reading process:

● Understands how print is organized and read
● Creates mental images from pictures and print
● Uses meaning clues to aid comprehension and make predictions about content

Uses reading skills and strategies to understand and interpret a variety of literary texts:

● Uses reading skills and strategies to understand a variety of familiar literary passages and texts, including fiction
● Knows main ideas or theme, setting, main characters, main events, sequence, and problems in stories
● Makes simple inferences regarding the order of events and possible outcomes
● Relates stories to personal experiences

Uses the general skills and strategies of the writing process:

● Uses writing and other methods to describe familiar persons, places, objects, or experiences
● Writes in a variety of forms or genres, including responses to literature

Source: *A Compendium of Standards and Benchmarks for K–12 Education* (Mid-Continent Regional Educational Laboratory, 1995)

Kevin Henkes

Born November 27, 1960; Racine, Wisconsin
Home: Madison, Wisconsin

Introduce your author study by inviting children to share what they already know about Kevin Henkes and to name the books with which they are familiar. Help children locate Kevin Henkes's home state on a map or globe. Then read aloud the following interview or share selected portions of it, and continue with any of the introductory activities on pages 8–12.

For writers, the creative process differs with the demands of each book. Few can point to a map and say, "This is exactly how I get there, every time." But despite the differences, patterns do emerge. For Kevin Henkes (HENG-kiss), the genesis of a book often begins with a character. The story line then naturally flows out of that character. In other words, the story can be seen as a revelation of the character. Kevin explains, "I almost always have the character first. The only way a book can be real, for me, is to have the character first and then take the story from there."

This should come as no surprise to Kevin's fans. For nearly twenty years (about half of his life!), Kevin Henkes has created a long list of endearing characters is his enduring books: Lilly and Sheila Rae, Wemberly and Chester, Owen and Chrysanthemum. In fact, the very titles themselves illustrate Kevin's "character first" approach. The stories are quiet, warm, funny and perceptive, and feature calm, realistic portrayals of children's lives.

Still, it's not as if fully-formed characters come knocking on Kevin's door, ready to appear in books. Developing a character, Kevin says, is a process of discovery. He compares it to slowly bringing an image into sharper focus before taking a photograph. He says, "When I am first thinking about characters, they are kind of cloudy. As I think about them—and maybe come to love them—little by little they come into focus. I think what brings them into focus is their particulars. For example, with Wemberly, I wanted it to be a kid who worried. That's fine and good, but when it started working was when I decided that she would have a spot over one eye, and one ear would be spotted, and when I decided that she would have some kind of object that she loved and carried around with her." There has to be "emotional truth," Kevin says, but also "physical details that are sharp and interesting—that's what makes the character unique."

Kevin continues, "I don't mention in *Chester's Way* that Lilly wears boots or a crown or a cape. But those were the details that came to me before I had put words on the page. Those were the things that make me want to write about her. It's those details that make a character interesting."

Part of the reason why Kevin's characters appear so complete is because he realizes that characters must have depth, including flaws and imperfections. "If a character is not fully developed," Kevin offers, "then that character will be flat and dull. That's why, in *Sheila Rae, the Brave*, she was brave...but she wasn't. And her sister Louise was not brave...but she was. I remember wanting to show Sheila Rae crying. I thought that helped make her a more believable, well-rounded character."

As a child, Kevin was always drawing. He recalls, "I knew I would be an artist." Along with his passion for art, Kevin also loved to write. Picture books, he discovered early on, allowed him to combine those two talents.

"It's always the story that comes first," Kevin claims. "You can be the world's best painter, but you may not be able to create a picture book. Today so many picture books are just decorative. But the art form of the picture book is, in fact, all thirty-two pages of pictures and words working together."

"I'll write the story, and that can take anywhere from a week to two months. When I write a picture book, I don't like to force anything. I write three lines, and that may take three hours. But I'll sit there and just doodle if I have to. Usually, I'll have the opening, and I'll know where I want to end up; working on the middle takes the most time."

Kevin, a father of two, draws upon his own childhood for inspiration. He does not describe specific events exactly, but recalls the emotions he experienced. That often provides the core of truth in his books. Kevin laughs, "That's the gift (or curse!) of being an artist and a writer. Before I had children—and I'd been doing this for years—people would often ask, 'How many children do you have?' I would say 'None.' And they would be amazed by that. Then when I became a parent, people would say, 'Oh, now you are going to have so many more ideas.' And, well, I think I learned what I had known all along: You don't need to have a child to write for children. It comes from within. It's something that I have and I don't know where it came from. But I do remember those feelings—very, very clearly."

He muses, "When I was young, I thought that if a person was going to be an author, then they needed to have done extraordinary things, traveled around the world, and had great adventures. But if you're a writer, then...you're a writer. No matter how humble your life may be, we all have stories to tell."

> "Just because I'm a published author doesn't mean that I don't make lots and lots of mistakes. It doesn't just happen naturally, even if you are good at something. It's hard work."
>
> —**Kevin Henkes**

Profile of Kevin Henkes from *The Big Book of Picture-Book Authors & Illustrators*, by James Preller (Scholastic Professional Books, 2001). Reprinted by permission of James Preller. Photo of Kevin Henkes courtesy of Tom Beckley/HarperCollins.

Teaching Activities for Any Time

Enhance and extend students' learning experiences with any Kevin Henkes book—or all of them—with the following ideas.

Story Charts

Explore story structure with a chart that lets students summarize information on characters, plot, setting, problem, and solution. Create a chart for each book you read. Guide children in using the charts to make connections between the books. For example, do students notice similarities in any of the settings? (See page 64 for a culminating activity that uses these charts.)

Individual Story Charts

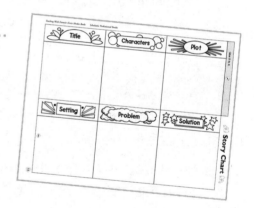

Use the template on page 13 to have children make individual story charts. You can photocopy the chart as is, or try these variations:

◉ Fill out a few of the story element boxes with information from the story. Have students use their knowledge of the story to complete the blank boxes.

◉ Fill out a few of the story element boxes with information from the story. Have students add new information to the blank boxes to create a new story.

To make stand-up charts, guide children in cutting out and gluing the sections as indicated. Then have them fill in the information and accordion-fold their charts. Stand the charts on a flat surface, such as a tabletop or counter.

Same Characters, Different Stories

Have students use their knowledge of story elements to make up new stories for book characters. Divide the class into groups. Give each group a copy of page 13. Invite students to choose a character, and then complete the form to plan a new story. Have students use the form as a guide for writing their story. Later, invite each group to act out its story for the class. To extend this idea, have children illustrate their stories, creating covers and title pages. In preparation, encourage them to examine several of Kevin Henkes's book covers and title pages. Have them think about how the art relates to the story and note the different letter styles or fonts.

What if...

Explain to children that any of the stories could have taken a different direction with a simple change or a different choice made by a character. For example, invite students to share their creative predictions about the following situations:

What if:

◎ Chester and Wilson were bullies?

◎ Lilly was not brave?

◎ Louise did not follow Sheila Rae?

◎ Ruthie did not meet a real Jessica?

◎ Sophie's parents called Wendell's parents?

◎ Mr. Slinger had not written a note to Lilly?

◎ Wemberly did not meet Jewel?

Story Card Activities

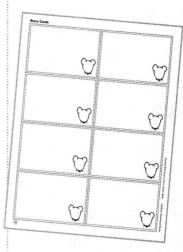

Copy the story cards on page 14 for use in the following activities:

◎ To make a game board, label each card on the page with an event from a story. Invite students, in turn, to toss a plastic jug lid onto the game board and act out the event on which it lands.

Tip
▲▲▲▲▲▲

Compare the features of the mouse characters. Ask children to point out features that distinguish recurring characters—such as Lilly—from the others.

◉ Randomly label each card on the page with an event from a story. Make a copy of the page for each student. Have children cut apart the cards, sequence them, and label the mouse shapes (in the lower right corners) with the corresponding numeral.

◉ Invite children to draw or write different events from a story in each card on the page. Ask them to number the cards according to the story sequence. Then have them cut apart and staple the sequenced cards between two decorated construction-paper covers. Have them share their resulting booklets with classmates and family.

◉ Label each card with an event from a story. Cut out the cards and tape them to separate paper lunch bags. Label the bag bottoms with numerals that correspond to the story sequence. To make the bags free standing, stuff each one with crumpled paper and fold down the top. Have children sequence the bags to create a story time line. After checking the sequence by looking at the number on the bottom of each bag, students can use the bags to retell the story.

Tip
▲▲▲▲▲

To make individual photo albums, give students multiple copies of page 15. Have them bind their album pages between construction-paper covers. Students can take home their photo albums and use them to share favorite parts of Kevin Henkes's stories with their families.

Exploring Characters

Photo Albums

As part of your character study, invite children to create a class picture album or "photo" display of Kevin Henkes's memorable characters. Simply have children draw the character of their choice on the photo album template. (See page 15.) If there are some characters who are not represented among children's choices, you might ask volunteers to create additional album pages. Have children complete the written portion of the page, then assemble the pages in a photo album or on a bulletin board display.

Character Charades

How well do your students know the characters of Kevin Henkes? Find out with a game of Character Charades. Whisper a character name to a volunteer. Then have the child silently act out the character's role as the class tries to guess the identity of the character. As an alternative—or if necessary—give clues to help children identify the character.

Secret Identity

Give students' knowledge about characters a workout with this fun group activity. Divide the class into groups. Tape the name of a character to the back of a volunteer in each group, without revealing the character to the child. Have the child turn to show his or her group members the character name. Then challenge the group to give clues to the child to help him or her guess the secret identity of the character.

Pen Pals

Ask children to name some of the characters they would like to know. Then have students write letters to those characters to express their desire to meet them. Encourage them to include information about themselves in the letters. Afterward, invite children to read their pen pal letters to the class. If desired, pretend to be the addressed character and verbally respond to the letter.

Common Characteristics

Children easily identify with many of Kevin Henkes's characters, but to which does each child identify most closely? Have each child draw that character on one end of a large sheet of paper. Have children create a self-portrait on the opposite end. In the middle of the page, have children list the characteristics that they have in common with the story character. Invite children to share their pictures with classmates.

Character Sort

Have students list the characters, then sort them into two categories by age (older and younger). Ask students to explain their reasons for the various placements. Then challenge children to estimate the ages of some of the characters. Use each response as a springboard to discuss whether or not the behavior and activities of each character are age-appropriate.

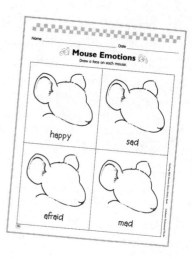

Exploring Emotions

Mouse Emotions

Kevin Henkes's characters show many different emotions. Ask children to examine how these emotions are represented in the illustrations. Then have students draw similar faces on the mice on page 16, matching each expression to the labeled emotion. Later, while sharing a story of your choice, have children point to each picture that matches the emotion a designated character experiences.

Emotions Wheel

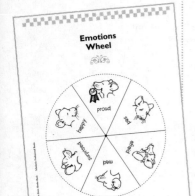

Make emotions wheels to explore feelings. Give each child a copy of page 17 and a small white paper plate. Cut an opening from a paper plate, as shown, to serve as a tracer. Help children trace and cut out similar openings in their paper plates. Have them color and cut out the wheel, and then use brass fasteners to attach them to the back of their paper plates. Children can use their wheels in any of the following activities:

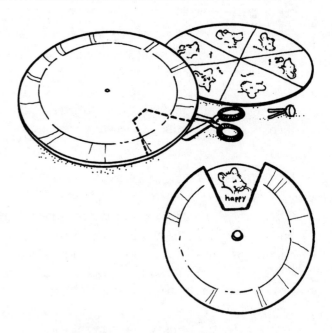

◎ Ask children to turn their wheels to any emotion. Have each child describe a story event in which a character felt that emotion.

◎ Turn your wheel to an emotion. Then ask children to turn their wheels to the matching emotion. Have them describe times they've experienced a similar feeling.

◎ Describe a situation (real, imaginary, or from a story). Ask children to turn their wheels to show how they might feel in that situation. Discuss their responses.

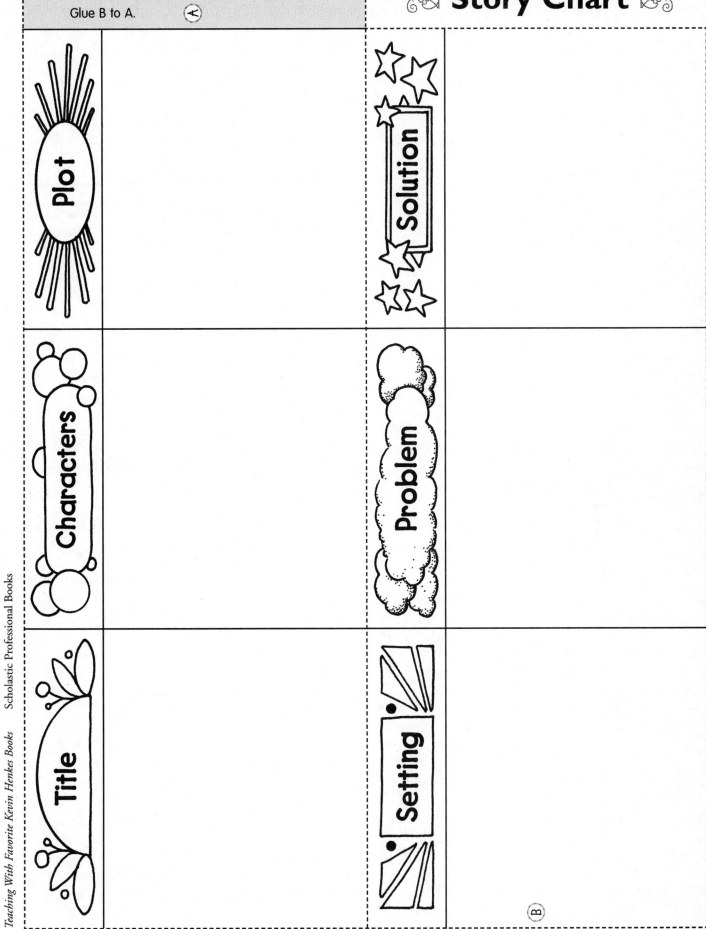

Glue B to A. (A)

Plot

Characters

Title

Solution

Problem

Setting

Teaching With Favorite Kevin Henkes Books   Scholastic Professional Books

(B)

Story Cards

Teaching With Favorite Kevin Henkes Books   Scholastic Professional Books

Photo Album

$\mathcal{M}$y name is _____.

My family members are _____

_____.

My friends are _____

_____.

I'm special because _____

_____.

I like _____

_____.

Read about me in _____.

Mouse Emotions

Draw a face on each mouse.

happy

sad

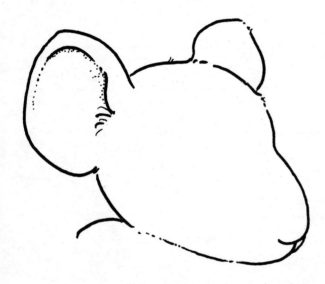

afraid

mad

Teaching With Favorite Kevin Henkes Books   Scholastic Professional Books

Emotions Wheel

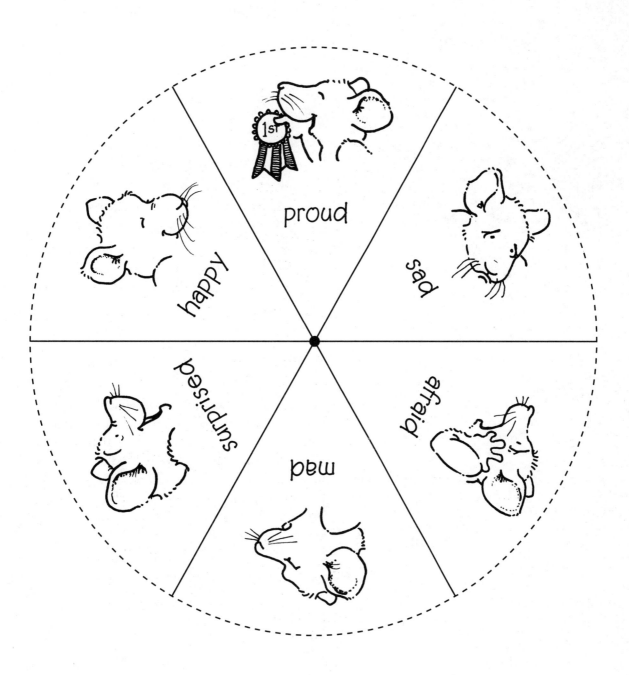

Owen

(GREENWILLOW BOOKS, 1993)

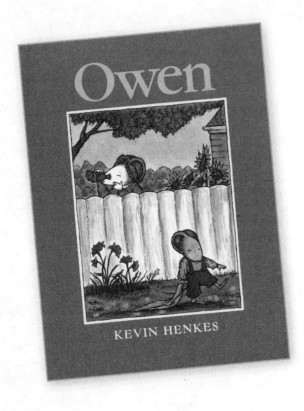

KEVIN HENKES

Oh, how Owen loves Fuzzy, the yellow blanket that he has had since he was a baby. But his neighbor, Mrs. Tweezers, thinks that Owen is too old for a blanket. On her advice, Owen's parents try time after time to separate their child from his beloved Fuzzy. Each attempt results in frustration for the parents and, finally, distress for Owen. Then his mother comes up with a brilliant idea—a creative solution that satisfies Owen and his parents, as well as the overly-concerned Mrs. Tweezers.

Messages and Themes

▲▲▲▲▲

◆ A person of any age might feel an attachment to a special childhood object.

◆ A problem may have many different solutions.

Owen certainly was attached to his yellow fuzzy blanket! After reading the story, pass around a small, fuzzy blanket. Invite each youngster to feel the blanket—to wrap it, twist it, and hug it—as if he or she were Owen. Then ask children to share their thoughts about how and why Owen became so attached to his blanket. Their responses might include the ideas that Owen's blanket made him feel safe or that he liked its color or its softness against his skin. To conclude your discussion, poll youngsters to find out how many feel that starting school marks the ideal time for Owen to give up his blanket.

Attachment Experiences (Language Arts)

Ask children to silently think about their own experiences with special items to which they are (or have been) attached, such as teddy bears, pajamas, or pillows. Follow up by having children anonymously draw the objects of their attachment on half-sheets of paper. Then ask them to write about how they feel about their items. Be sure to draw and write about your own personal experience, especially if you have a childhood item that remains special to you even now. Place the pages into a shoe box, then cover the box with a small blanket.

Reach under the blanket and pull pages out of the box one at a time to share with students. Contributors might wish to identify themselves and to tell more about their experiences. As students share, reassure them that having an attachment to a special object is not uncommon. Explain that even after one's attachment to the item fades, the object may continue to be special to that person for a long, long time.

Story Strips (Language Arts)

To demonstrate Owen's attachment to his blanket, share the pictures on the second page of the story. Explain that Owen has Fuzzy with him in each activity. Then page through the rest of the book to find other activities in which Owen includes Fuzzy. Let children create fold-out story strips to show how they might include favorite items in their daily activities.

◎ Have children cut 9- by-12-inch sheets of white construction paper in half lengthwise, and then tape the halves together end-to-end to make one long strip.

◎ Direct students to accordion-fold their strips into six four-inch-wide sections. Ask them to title the top section "Me and My (name of item)."

◎ Have children fill in the remaining sections with pictures of themselves engaged in the different activities with their special objects.

Explore Emotions

Special childhood items—such as blankets—can make children feel safe and secure, remind them of good times and loving people, or simply reassure them that everything in the world is fine. When children face separation from their special objects, they may feel anxiety along with a mixture of other emotions, such as sadness, fear, or anger. Invite students to tell about their feelings during their own separation experiences.

The Flavor Corner (Science)

Yuck! Owen's dad dipped the corner of Fuzzy in vinegar! Why? To help children arrive at an answer, pour some vinegar into a cup. Invite each child to dip one end of a craft stick into the vinegar and then taste it. Record their comments and reactions on chart paper. Then have students discuss why Owen's dad flavored his blanket with vinegar. To extend this idea, invite children to taste various foods preserved in vinegar, such as cucumbers (pickles) or a vegetable mix. They might also dip celery sticks in vinegar-based sauces such as mustard, barbecue sauce, and salad dressings. Which vinegar-based flavor is their favorite?

How Many Hankies? (Math)

Strengthen estimation and measurement skills with this activity. Explain that Owen's mother probably measured and estimated the number of handkerchiefs that she could make from his blanket before she began to snip and sew. To demonstrate the process she might have followed, divide the class into small groups. Give each group a 36-inch square of paper and several four-inch construction-paper squares. Tell students that the large square represents a blanket, and the small ones represent handkerchiefs. Ask them to use the small squares to estimate the number of handkerchiefs that they can make from the paper blanket. Have children write their estimates on sticky notes and then post them on a sheet of chart paper. To check their guesses, ask children to cut out four-inch paper hankies, then fit them neatly together to cover the blanket. Have them count the handkerchiefs, then compare their estimates with the actual results.

Dear Blanket Fairy
(Language Arts)

Have students speculate what the big-boy gift for Owen might have been. Ask them to name some items that the Blanket Fairy might leave them to replace their special blankets. Then invite children to glue or draw pictures and write their names on the blanket pattern. (See page 22.) After students share their pages with the class, display them on a fabric-covered bulletin board representing a blanket.

(See page 22.)

Explore Emotions

Find the page in the book on which Owen's parents tell him "No." Point out the large picture on the wall. Explain that it is an imitation of a famous painting known as "The Scream" by Edvard Munch. How does it represent Owen's feelings at that moment? Ask children to share their thoughts about why Kevin Henkes might have included this painting in this illustration. Invite students to paint self-portraits showing how they might feel in Owen's position. Or have them write about times when they experienced similar feelings.

At the Dentist's Office (Social Studies/Dramatic Play)

Remind students that Owen even took his blanket to the dentist. A visit to the dentist may be a new and anxiety-producing experience for some of your students. Ask children who have visited the dentist to share their experiences. Then set up a dentist office in your dramatic play area to introduce children to a few simple dental tools and procedures.

Personalized Blankets (Art)

From juice stains to spots worn thin from sucking, hugging, and twisting, Fuzzy bore all the signs of belonging uniquely to Owen. Ask children to imagine that they own special blankets. What do the blankets look like? What characteristics identify each blanket as belonging to its owner? Provide students with 18-inch squares of muslin and a variety of craft items, such as fabric paint, lace trim, ribbon, large plastic needles, and embroidery thread. Invite them to design and decorate the squares to represent their own unique blankets. Later, ask children to tell about their blankets, then display them on a bulletin board. Or have children use their blankets in the movement activity below.

Musical Blankets (Music/Movement)

Show students the pictures of Owen on the inside covers of the book. What is he doing? Lead children to conclude that he and Fuzzy are moving around in creative ways—after all, Owen and Fuzzy did everything together! To engage children in some similar creative movement, play a variety of styles of music—from soft, flowing selections to music with a steady, rhythmic beat. During each selection, invite students to dance and move in creative and expressive ways using their blankets (from the Personalized Blankets activity above). Students could also use handkerchiefs or scarves as blankets.

Book Links

D.W.'s Lost Blankie
by Marc Brown
(Little, Brown, 1998)

After an all-day search for her lost blankie, sad D.W. goes to bed empty-handed. And, try as she might, sleep just won't come. That is, until Mother arrives to save the night!

Franklin's Blanket
by Paulette Bourgeois
(Kids Can Press Ltd., 1997)

Franklin sulks all day over the loss of his misplaced blanket. Then an odd odor jogs his memory, and he finds his blanket right where he had left it—filled with day-old brussel sprouts!

Dear Blanket Fairy,

Take my blanket. Take it, please.
But when you do, leave one of these!

Love, _____

Teaching With Favorite Kevin Henkes Books   Scholastic Professional Books

Chrysanthemum

(GREENWILLOW BOOKS, 1991)

Chrysanthemum. What an absolutely perfect name! Just the sight and sound of it made Chrysanthemum bloom. But when school starts and her classmates make fun of her name, poor Chrysanthemum wilts with embarassment. In an unexpected turn of events, though, her peers discover that having a flower name is really quite special— and Chrysanthemum once again blossoms with pride.

Invite children to express their opinions about Chrysanthemum's name. Then ask them to share their feelings about their own names.

Extend the Book

Flower Characters (Language Arts)

Creativity will bloom when children invent these special characters. To begin, help students generate a list of flower names. Ask them to choose names from the list and then develop and illustrate characters for their name choices. Encourage children to describe their characters and explain why their chosen names are absolutely perfect. Later, display the character drawings and descriptions on a class bulletin board.

Messages and Themes

▲▲▲▲▲▲

◆ A person's name is part of his or her individuality.

◆ Kind words breed good feelings and friendship. Unkind words are hurtful.

◆ Parents and teachers can offer support and understanding during times of trouble.

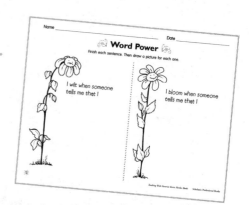

Tip

▲▲▲▲▲

For a fun and confidence-building display, cut out flowers and label them with words and phrases that help children "bloom."

Thank-You Cards (Language Arts)

Chrysanthemum's parents were very supportive during her difficult times. Encourage children to recall ways in which parents, caretakers, or others have supported them. Have them make cards to express their thanks to these special people.

Word Power (Language Arts)

Explain the words *wilted* and *bloomed* as they are used in the story. Give each child a copy of page 27. Have children write endings to the two phrases, then illustrate each statement. Invite them to share their pictures with the class.

Blooming Flower Puppets (Art/Language Arts)

Watch children blossom with this activity. Give each child a copy of the flower pattern on page 28. Ask children to cut out the flowers, paste or draw pictures of themselves in the space indicated, then attach construction paper leaves and craft-stick stems. Have students fold their flower petals over their pictures. To make their flowers bloom, children simply unfold the petals until their pictures are exposed. To extend the activity, invite small groups to name kind things about a classmate for each petal that he or she opens.

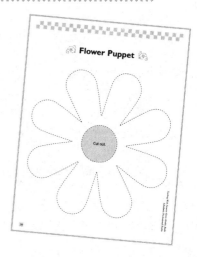

Words in a Name (Language Arts)

Long names, such as *Chrysanthemum*, are absolutely perfect sources from which to create shorter words. To help children make new words, cut out 13 paper petals, label each with a letter from *Chrysanthemum*, and arrange them to make a flower. Then invite children to pick the flower petals and sequence them to create new words. To extend the activity, invite children to use the letters from *Victoria* or *Delphinium* to create new words.

Names Count (Math)

How many syllables are in *Chrysanthemum*? To find out, clap and count the syllables while saying the name with students. In the same manner, count and then graph students' names according to the syllable count. Compare the results to find the names with the most and fewest syllables. If desired, graph students' names according to the letter count. Use the graph to determine which children have the longest and shortest names.

Weather Moods (Art/Social Studies)

Point out how Kevin Henkes uses the environment and weather to reinforce Chrysanthemum's moods. For example, during her happy days, the sun is shining, the sky is blue, and butterflies are fluttering around. But during her sad moods, rain falls, the sky is dark, and lightning flashes. Challenge children to create environmental pictures to depict different moods they've experienced, beginning, for example, with how they felt when they woke up this morning!

Pockets Full of Prizes (Art/Language Arts)

One day before going to school, Chrysanthemum loaded her seven pockets with good-luck charms and prized possessions. Invite children to make a shirt full of good-luck pockets with this activity. First, ask them to cut shirts from large sheets of construction paper. Then have them glue gift-wrap pockets to their shirts. (NOTE: Have students place glue along bottom and side edges only.) For each pocket on their shirts, have students draw and cut out a good-luck charm or a prized possession. Have them slip the drawings into their shirt pockets. Later, invite children to share their pictures with the class, taking them out of the pockets one at a time.

Josephina Hates Her Name

by Diana Engel (Morrow Junior Books, 1989)

Josephina hates her ugly, unusual name until she discovers that it came from a special relative.

A Porcupine Named Fluffy

by Helen Lester (Houghton Mifflin, 1986)

Fluffy the porcupine and a rhinoceros named Hippo find humor and acceptance in their unique names.

Alison's Zinnia

by Anita Lobel (Greenwillow, 1990)

Clever text combined with colorful illustrations of 26 young girls and their floral finds fill this book with alphabetical appeal.

Floral Fun (Science/Math)

Gather a supply of silk or real flowers. Ask children to examine the flowers to identify the different parts of each: stem, leaves, petals, stamens, and pistils. Then invite them to draw a floral scene, using the flowers as models. For an extension to the activity, place the flowers in a learning center. Challenge children to sort the flowers by different attributes, such as size or color. Have them count and compare the number of flowers in each group.

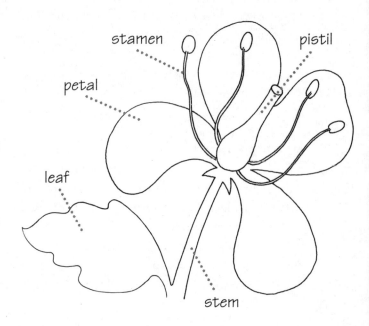

Mapping the Way (Social Studies)

By the third day, dejected Chrysanthemum slowly worked her way to school by taking the longest route possible. Do your students know the way from their homes to school? Ask them to draw maps showing the routes. If possible, mark the school's location on a map of your community. Help children find their streets on the map and trace the route to school.

Name _____

Date _____

Word Power

Finish each sentence. Then draw a picture for each one.

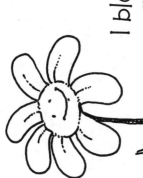

I bloom when someone
tells me that I

· ·

I wilt when someone
tells me that I

Teaching With Favorite Kevin Henkes Books   Scholastic Professional Books

Flower Puppet

Cut out.

Teaching With Favorite Kevin Henkes Books
Scholastic Professional Books

A Weekend With Wendell

(GREENWILLOW BOOKS, 1986)

When Wendell spends the weekend, Sophie and her parents find that their hospitality—and patience—is pushed to the limit. Not only are Wendell's pranks and antics hard to bear, but his insensitive behavior toward Sophie is hurtful. That is, until the kind but clever Sophie gives Wendell a dose of his own medicine! Afterward, an unlikely friendship develops.

Discuss with children how Sophie and Wendell enjoyed each other's company when they played cooperatively with the water hose. Have them compare this situation to earlier ones in which Wendell made all the rules or acted inconsiderately. How did Wendell's behavior make Sophie feel? Lead children to understand that turn-taking, cooperation, and consideration are all part of fair play and being a good friend.

Messages and Themes

◆ Cooperation and fair play make sleepovers fun for everyone.

◆ Conflicts can be resolved in fun, creative ways.

◆ The positive resolution to a conflict can lead to a good, strong friendship.

Explore Emotions

Invite children to tell about some of the cooperative activities as well as conflicts that might have occurred during their sleepover experiences. How did they feel during each situation? If children experienced conflicts during a sleepover, ask them to describe how the conflict was resolved and what their feelings were afterward.

Tip

▲▲▲▲▲

Sophie wrote a note to her friend Wendell. Invite children to write notes to their friends. (Check to make sure everyone will get a note.)

Alliteration Creations   (Language Arts)

Point out the title of the book. Guide children to realize that most of the title words begin with the same letter—*w*. Explain that this is called *alliteration*. Then ask students to make up alliterative titles using their names. Afterward, challenge them to create short stories to fit their titles.

Sorted and Packed to Go

(Language Arts/Critical Thinking)

Categorization skills are packed to go in this booklet activity. To begin, ask children to separate an assortment of clothing, personal items, and toys into different stacks. Discuss why each item belongs in the stack into which it was sorted. Then ask children to color, cut out, fold, and write their names on the booklet cover on page 33. To make pages, have children staple a stack of half-sheets of paper inside the cover. Ask children to label different sections of their booklets with category names, such as clothes, personal things, and toys to represent the types of things they might pack for a sleepover. Then have them draw corresponding items in each section. Later, let children use their books to share the contents of their sleepover bags with the class.

Three-Part Drama (Dramatic Arts/Social Studies)

Wendell acted out several simultaneous roles during his play activities with Sophie. Challenge children to give their drama skills a similar workout with this activity. Write a set of three related roles—such as doctor, nurse, and patient—on one note card along with a situation involving the three roles. After creating several cards in this manner, place each one in a separate envelope. Invite children, in groups of three, to randomly select the envelopes, silently read the enclosed cards, and then act out all the roles for the given situations. Encourage the rest of the class to guess each situation being represented and the different roles involved in it.

Which Wendell? (Critical Thinking)

Sophie and her parents knew that the one-and-only Wendell was responsible for the melted crayons, peanut butter and jelly paintings, and toothpaste-covered mirrors at their house. But, in this guessing game, do your students know which "Wendell" has the missing crayon? To play, place a crayon and paper on a table. Assign one child to be Sophie and the rest of your class the role of Wendell. As Sophie covers her eyes, appoint one Wendell to take the crayon and hide it on himself or herself. Then invite Sophie to guess which Wendell took the crayon. Each time she makes an incorrect guess, have the child she named give her a clue about the Wendell with the missing crayon, such as eye color or first initial of his or her name. When Sophie finally guesses correctly, ask the identified Wendell to sign his or her real name to the paper. Repeat as long as student interest allows.

When Did It Happen? (Math)

It seems that Wendell had some very busy days at Sophie's house! To discover what time of day different events happened, ask children to complete page 34. Simply have them cut out the row of boxes at the bottom of the page, refer to the book to determine when each described event happened, and then glue the corresponding box to the appropriate space.

Tip

▲▲▲▲▲

List appropriate behaviors for the host and guest of an overnight visit. Invite children to act out these roles in their dramatic play activities.

Tip

▲▲▲▲▲

Check for food allergies before serving samples of green foods.

Book Links

Bootsie Barker Bites
by Barbara Bottner
(Putnam, 1992)

On learning that the bullying Bootsie Barker is to spend the night, a clever young hostess invents a game to end her guest's undesirable ways.

Everything to Spend the Night
by Ann Whitford Paul
(Dorling Kindersley, 1999)

Whether children are planning a sleepover with grandparents or with friends, this alphabet book is stuffed with ideas about fun things to pack in their overnight bags.

Yummy Greens (Math)

Do students really believe that Wendell was allergic to green foods? After discussing their opinions, invite children to sample a variety of green foods. Then have them cast ballots to indicate their food preferences from the available choices. Count the votes to discover which green food is the class favorite.

"Sense-ational" Centers (Creative Expression)

Review the different kinds of multisensory activities in which Wendell engaged, such as fingerpainting with food, writing with toothpaste, creating a hairdo with shaving cream, and playing in the water. Set up several centers with similar sensory materials, discuss appropriate behavior and uses for each center, then invite children to engage in some cooperative creative expression at the centers.

_____'s

Sleepover Bag

When Did It Happen?

Read each sentence. Decide what time of day each event happened.
Cut out a picture that shows that time of day. Glue it on the box.

◎ Wendell's parents
take him to Sophie's
house.

◎ Sophie finds a note
from Wendell on her
pillow.

◎ During lunch, Wendell
fingerpaints with
peanut butter and jelly.

◎ Wendell pinches
Sophie's leg
at breakfast.

◎ Wendell shines
a flashlight
in Sophie's eyes.

◎ Wendell tries to
make a long-
distance phone call.

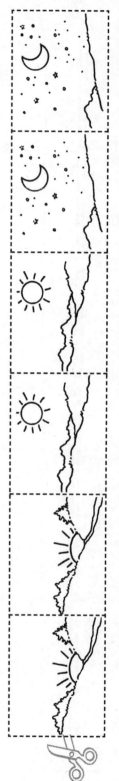

*Teaching With
Favorite Kevin
Henkes Books*
Scholastic
Professional
Books

Sheila Rae, the Brave

(GREENWILLOW BOOKS, 1987)

Sheila Rae's bravery leads her along a new path home from school. But, caught up in her courageous curiosity, she suddenly discovers that she is lost. Frightened Sheila Rae calls out for help, and she's answered by her "scaredy-cat" sister, Louise. In an unexpected moment of courage, Louise guides her brave older sister back home, demonstrating that they are both quite fearless.

Sheila Rae is truly a brave child! Discuss with children her many courageous acts. Then help them point out some of her unwise actions. Lead students to understand that taking an unknown path was not a wise choice—and might possibly have become dangerous. Have children share some wise choices that Sheila Rae might have made instead, such as taking the familiar path, telling an adult about her plans, or walking with a friend who was familiar with her chosen route.

Messages and Themes

▲▲▲▲▲

◆ Family members can help keep each other safe.

◆ Sometimes being brave calls for making wise and cautious choices.

◆ To avoid getting lost, use familiar routes and paths.

Extend the Book

Pick a Path (Social Studies)

For a little variety, brave Sheila Rae took a different route home. Add variety to students' daily routines by taking different routes to familiar places, such as the cafeteria, computer lab, and media center. Ask children to compare the new and familiar routes. Periodically, invite them to vote for and then take their preferred route to a designated location.

On the Way With Sheila Rae

(Social Studies/Sequencing)

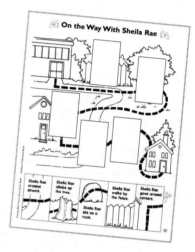

Invite students to help Sheila Rae retrace her path with this map. To begin, make a copy of page 39 for each child. Have children cut out the bottom row of boxes. Then have them glue the boxes in the appropriate spaces on the map to indicate the sequence of Sheila Rae's route.

Stroll Scrolls (Language Arts/Social Studies)

Sheila Rae's walk took her past many sights. Take children on a stroll around the school area. Back in the room, have children illustrate long strips of paper with some of the sights from their walk. Ask children to write or dictate descriptive statements about their pictures. Have them roll their strips into scrolls and tie them with ribbon. Invite small groups to share their scrolls and walking experiences with the class.

Picture-Perfect Qualities (Language Arts/Art)

Sheila Rae was brave and active. Louise was quiet and cautious. Ask children to think of words that describe their best qualities, such as *energetic, kind, honest,* and *strong*. Then let them make personalized picture magnets to represent these strengths. Have children cut out construction-paper picture frames. Ask them to write their descriptive words on the frames and decorate them with craft items such as glitter and sequins. Have children glue the frames around their photos (or self-portraits), back them with tagboard, and trim the backing to the shape of the frame. Finally, have them attach magnetic tape to the back of their frames.

Sidewalk Math (Math)

Stepping on sidewalk cracks was one way that Sheila Rae showed off her bravery. Invite children to step into some measurement practice with this activity. Assign small groups a specific number of sidewalk cracks (or tile lines on the floor). Ask them to use standard or nonstandard units to measure the distance between the first and last cracks. Then record their findings on a chart. Later, compare and discuss the results.

Map It Out (Social Studies)

Give children enlarged maps of your school. Have them use different-colored markers to draw the routes from their classroom to each different location in their weekly routine. If desired, invite students to create corresponding color keys for their maps. For example, children might use red for Music, indicating that the red line on their maps marks the route to music class.

Book Links

Franklin Is Lost

by Paulette Bourgeois
(Kids Can Press, 1992)

When Franklin gets lost in the woods, the tired and frightened turtle curls up into his shell to wait. What joy he feels when he finally hears someone call his name!

Arthur Lost and Found

by Marc Brown
(Little, Brown, 1998)

On the bus ride to the pool, Arthur falls asleep and misses his stop. Although lost and worried, he figures out just what to do and is soon back home with his relieved family.

Mystery Trail (Language Arts/Social Studies)

After all of her skipping, climbing, and backward-walking, Sheila Rae discovered that her location was quite a mystery. But when you create this fun mystery route, the final stop will hold a surprise—not a mystery—for students. Secretly plot a mystery route around your classroom or school. Hide clues at different landmarks along the route and a special treat at the end. To get children started on the route, give them the first clue. Challenge them to follow its message to discover the next clue. Have them continue in this manner until they reach the end of the route—and the surprise awaiting them!

Blue-Ribbon Bravery (Language Arts)

Sheila Rae seemed to like attention for her acts of bravery. Recognize your students' courage with this activity. To begin, invite children to share their acts of bravery with the class. Then have them describe and illustrate their experiences on paper. To award students for their bravery, affix blue ribbons

with large yellow smiley stickers to the papers. Display student work with a banner labeled "Blue-Ribbon Bravery."

Fancy Fences (Art)

Point out the graffiti on the fence in the book. Then have children accordion-fold and unfold long strips of paper to resemble fences. Invite them to decorate their paper fences with colorful graffiti. Stand the fences on shelves, window ledges, and other flat surfaces around the room.

On the Way With Sheila Rae

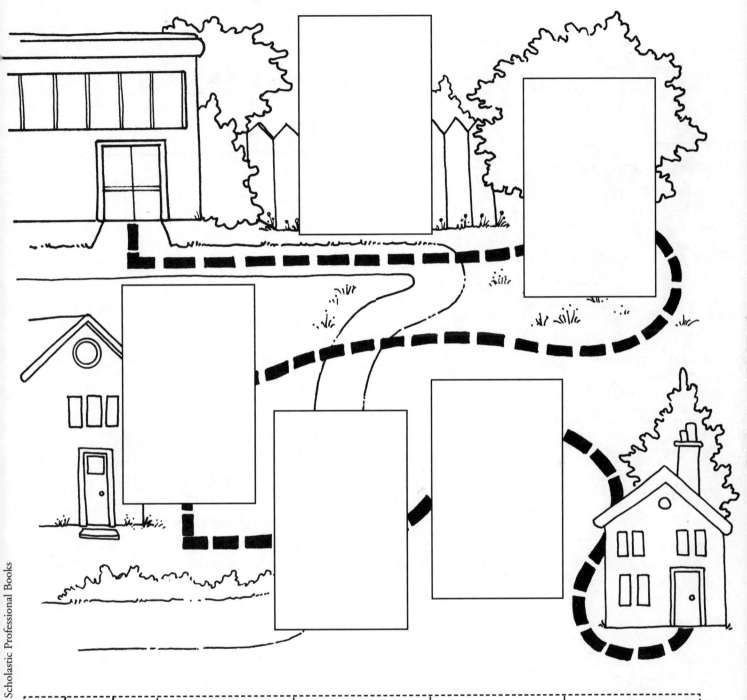

 Sheila Rae crosses streets.

Sheila Rae climbs up the tree.

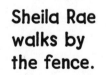 Sheila Rae sits on a rock.

Sheila Rae walks by the fence.

Sheila Rae goes around corners.

Chester's Way

(GREENWILLOW BOOKS, 1988)

Messages and Themes

▲▲▲▲▲

◆ Each individual has unique ways of doing things.

◆ Friendships result when we accept each other's similarities and differences.

◆ We can learn new and fun things from each other.

Chester has his own way of doing everything. His best friend, Wilson, is exactly the same way. They do everything together and everything alike—like two peas in a pod. Then the two friends meet Lilly. Lilly does things her own way. Because her ways are so different from their own, Chester and Wilson go out of their way to avoid Lilly. But when Lilly rescues the boys from an unpleasant dilemma, they discover that she's not really that different after all. Before long, the three friends are virtually inseparable.

Invite children to discuss the differences between Chester and Wilson and Lilly. Must people always be alike to be friends? Lead children to understand that the characters accepted each other's similarities and differences—and even learned that differences can be fun!

Friendship Creatures (Art/Language Arts)

The three friends created a large creature together. In the same spirit, have groups of two or three children cooperatively create Friendship Creature posters. Ask them to label the special characteristics of their creatures, such as "always smiles," "stars shine in eyes," "wears cheerful colors," and "uses hands to help others." Display the posters, then invite the groups to tell about their creatures.

Three Best Friends (Music)

On Halloween, the three friends dressed as the Three Blind Mice. Challenge children to create and sing a song titled "Three Best Friends" to the tune of this popular song. Or invite them to sing the following version in a class sing-along:

> Three best friends.
> Three best friends.
> Friends to the end.
> Friends to the end.
> They ride their bikes and swim in the pool.
> They like to talk backward so it sounds cool.
> They stick together 'cause that's the rule.
> Three best friends.

Tip

▲▲▲▲▲

For fun, ask children to write and say their names backward. Can they make up silly rhymes with their backward names?

Seeds of Thought (Science)

Discuss Wilson's fear about a watermelon plant growing inside him. Ask youngsters to share their thoughts about his concerns. Is it possible to grow a plant inside a person? Why or why not? Direct the discussion to include the basic needs of plants—soil, water, and light. Then invite children to plant and nurture a supply of fast-growing seeds.

Tip

▲▲▲▲▲

Do children think that Victor will be welcomed into the trio's friendship? Ask them to extend the story to include Victor.

Friendship Fun (Language Arts/Social Studies)

Explore friendship with children by having them complete some or all of these activities:

◉ Examine the friendship between Chester, Wilson, and Lilly. Then ask students to write characteristics of friendships on bulletin board paper. Have children decorate the paper with pictures of themselves and their friends engaged in a variety of activities. Display the Friendship Mural as a reminder of good-friend qualities.

◉ Have children make "Best Friend" posters to advertise themselves as good friends.

◉ Like the friendship between Chester, Wilson, and Lilly, many friendships last through the seasons. Have children divide large sheets of paper into quarters and then label each section with a different season. Ask them to draw pictures of themselves and friends enjoying activities related to the season in each section.

◉ Celebrate the similarities and differences found within friendships with this simple game. Label each of a supply of note cards with a sentence including an action and a phrase about students' interests or personal features, such as "If you have red hair, stomp three times" or "Shake hands with someone who likes to roller-blade." Put the notes in a basket. Have children take turns reading selected notes aloud. Encourage students to respond appropriately to each message.

Safety Signals (Health/Safety)

Often Chester and Wilson practiced using hand signals while riding their bikes. Invite children to use hand signals when they travel down the halls and around the school. Or set up an obstacle course with lots of turns, then have students practice their signals while negotiating the course.

Stopping/
Slowing Down

Right
Turn

Left
Turn

Nifty Disguises (Art/Language Arts)

Lilly gave Chester and Wilson nifty disguises for Christmas. Have children secretly create their own nifty disguises from an assortment of craft items and dress-up clothes. (They might page through the book for inspiration.) Then photograph small groups of disguised children together. Have them anonymously write clues about their disguises, then put their papers and the photo into a large envelope. During group time, read the papers one at a time. Show the photo after reading each paper, challenging the class to point out the child with the described disguise. Which child is hiding behind the disguise? Later, display the pictures and papers for additional enjoyment.

"Let's Share!" Math Mats
(Math)

The friendship in this story moved from a duo to a trio. Use these mats to illustrate how this change affects the quantity that the friends receive when they share certain things. Give each child a copy of the mat on page 44. Invite children to evenly divide sets of counters— such as bears, cereal squares, or paper clips— between the mice on one side of the mat. Have them count and label the amount for each mouse. Then instruct them to repeat the activity for the other side of the mat. Ask children to compare the labeled amounts on both sides of the mat.

Just-in-Case Kits (Science/Social Studies)

Chester always carried a small first-aid kit with him—just in case. Ask children to name some items that might be found in his kit. Then open a first-aid kit and examine its contents. Invite volunteers to explain the purpose of each item. (Or ask the school nurse to explain and demonstrate the use of the items.) Later, have children draw items that they might include in their own personal first-aid kits.

Book Links

Franklin's New Friend
by Paulette Bourgeois
(Kids Can Press, 1997)

Franklin is reluctant to be a buddy to his new neighbor and classmate, big Moose. But after spending a little time together, the two discover a very special friendship.

Odd Velvet
by Mary E. Whitcomb
(Chronicle Books, 1998)

While Velvet's classmates politely avoid her, they observe her odd ways with cautious curiosity. Little by little, her unique perspective on life begins to make sense, until even her toughest critic grows to accept and appreciate Velvet.

❧ Let's Share! ❧

Divide the items evenly between the mice.
Then count and write the numeral on the line.

How many? _____

How many? _____

How many? _____

❧ Let's Share! ❧

Divide the items evenly between the mice.
Then count and write the numeral on the line.

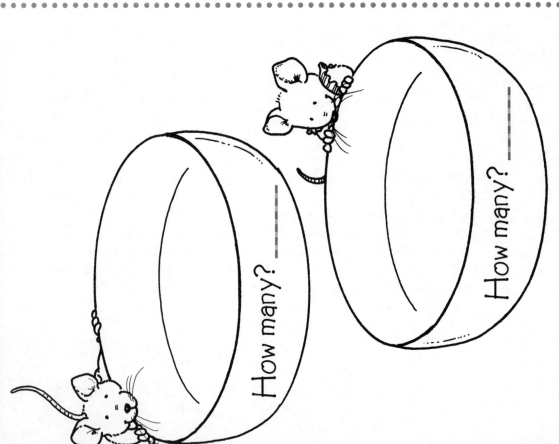

How many? _____

How many? _____

Julius, the Baby of the World

(GREENWILLOW BOOKS, 1990)

JULIUS
THE BABY OF THE WORLD

KEVIN HENKES

Lilly's loving enthusiasm for the new baby turns into mean-green jealousy after her brother arrives. She refuses to kiss, admire, and stroke baby Julius as her parents do. Instead, the disgusted Lilly pinches, insults, and wishes him away. Even extra attention, special privileges, and parental corrections can't change her attitude. But when cousin Garland expresses her disgust with the baby, Lilly's big-sister pride kicks in as she discovers that Julius holds a special place in her heart after all.

Lilly experienced a great deal of frustration and jealousy over her baby brother. Page through the book with your class and list behaviors that indicate these feelings. Ask children to discuss more positive ways in which Lilly might have behaved.

Messages and Themes

◆ It is natural for a child to feel jealousy over a new baby.

◆ Older siblings may need time to adjust to and accept a new baby.

◆ A new baby requires a lot of love, care, and attention from family members.

Explore Emotions

Explain that, at first, Lilly felt such big-sister pride. Then her pride gave way to jealousy, along with a host of other emotions including hate, anger, fear, sadness, and feeling rejected. Fortunately, Lilly rediscovered her big-sister pride! Invite children with younger siblings to share the feelings they experienced over their new babies. What other family situations and events might make them feel pride, jealousy, or any other emotion experienced by Lilly?

Tip

▲ ▲ ▲ ▲ ▲

Ask children to define germ. Was Julius really a germ? Use this discussion as a springboard to discuss personal hygiene.

Storytime Gestures (Language Arts)

Teach children simple gestures for the repetitive phrases about baby Julius. For example, they might point to their nose for "wet pink nose," point to eyes for "small black eyes," rub their stomach for "sweet white fur," and cradle imaginary babies for "baby of the world." Afterward, read the story again, encouraging children to use the appropriate gesture each time they hear one of the designated phrases.

Stop-and-Go Behaviors (Language Arts/Social Studies)

Use these stop-and-go signs to help children understand that there are more desirable, positive alternatives to Lilly's negative behaviors. To begin, have children write about or illustrate one of Lilly's undesirable behaviors on half-sheets of red paper. Then ask them to write or draw a more positive alternative to the behavior on half-sheets of green paper. Instruct children to glue their red and green pages back-to-back, inserting a wide craft stick handle between them. Then read the story again. Ask students to listen for the times when Lilly's behavior corresponds to their red signs. When they hear these parts, have students hold up their red pictures to request a pause in the story. Then invite them to share the positive alternative to Lilly's behavior on the green side of their signs.

Vocabulary Check (Language Arts)

Help children define the word *disgusting*. To what is Lilly referring when she uses this word? Did students find any of Lilly's actions or behaviors disgusting? Which ones? Why? Invite children to share stories about times in which their own behaviors might have been disgusting to others. Have them discuss acceptable alternatives to their disgusting behaviors.

Repeat the Positive (Language Arts/Social Studies)

Unlike Lilly, her parents always said positive things about baby Julius. Encourage children to practice similar positive phrasing with this idea. To begin, have them pick a favorite stuffed animal. Then ask them to generate positive descriptive phrases about their animals (such as those describing Julius in the story). Finally, encourage children to write about their animals, using the phrases repetitively throughout their stories. Display the stories and animals together so that students can share their work with each other.

Baby Days and School Days (Social Studies)

Because of their age difference, Lilly and Julius have very different needs. Ask children to compare the characters' needs. Why does Julius require so much more attention from their parents and other adults? Explain that older children are more independent and do not rely on adults like they did when they were babies. Let students make special booklets to compare their baby days and school days.

◉ Give each child multiple copies of page 50. Have children complete and illustrate the sentences to make pages for their books, then cut apart the pages.

◉ Have children stack the baby pages behind a half-sheet of construction paper labeled "Baby Days." Have them stack the remaining pages, in a corresponding sequence, behind a half-sheet of construction paper labeled "School Days."

◉ Show students how to staple the "Baby Days" stack to the left side of a full sheet of construction paper and the "School Days" to the right side of the paper. Invite them to glue a baby photo (or a drawing of themselves as a baby) to the left cover and a school photo (or drawing of themselves now) to the right cover.

Letters to Lilly (Language Arts)

For most of the story, the words and
behaviors that Lilly directs to her baby
brother are less than kind. Ask children to
imagine that they are Julius. Have them
write letters to Lilly describing how her
behavior and rejection makes them feel.
Encourage children to conclude their letters
by telling Lilly how they feel when she is
caring and kind toward them. To share the
letters, don a pair of boots and a disguise to
assume the role of Lilly. Invite students to
read their Julius letters to Lilly. Then have
Lilly respond with appropriate apologies
and pledges of better behavior.

Suitcase Share Time (Language Arts)

Remind students that Lilly ran away seven times in one morning. Did
running away resolve her problems? Discuss more appropriate alternatives
for Lilly—for example, talking about her problems with her parents, a
trusted adult, or a close friend. To reinforce this idea, ask children to label
folded sheets of paper "When I have a problem I…." On the inside, have
them complete and illustrate the sentence. Put the papers in a small suitcase.
During group time, share the pages one at a time with the class. If students
desire, invite them to tell more about their pictures.

Extra Time! (Math)

Lilly's parents allowed her to stay up 15 minutes later each night. To
reinforce this time concept, set a timer to give children an extra 15 minutes
to engage in activities of their choice. Or challenge them to remain engaged
in assigned activities—such as writing, reading, or math—for the designated
period of time. Discuss whether or not the extra time made the activities
more (or less) pleasurable.

Family Mobiles (Social Studies)

Many of Lilly's relatives came to the celebration in honor of Julius. Invite children to create these family mobiles to celebrate the members of their families. In advance, send home a parent request for names of students' closest relatives, such as their parents, siblings, grandparents, uncles, aunts, and cousins. Then have children trace gingerbread people shapes to represent the people on their lists (or provide pre-cut shapes). Ask them to cut out and label each shape with a corresponding name. Then have children tape yarn to the shapes, tie them to the rim of a paper plate (punch holes around the edge), and add yarn hangers. After sharing their mobiles with the class, invite students to display them at home for their families to enjoy.

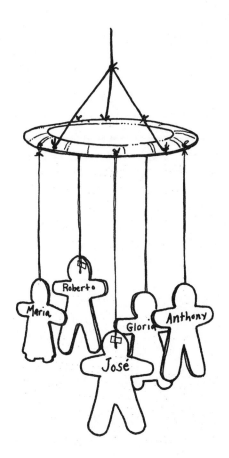

Book Links

She Come Bringing Me That Little Baby Girl

by Eloise Greenfield
(J.P. Lippincott, 1974)

The fuss everyone makes over the new baby girl just sickens Kevin, especially since he wanted a brother. But when his mother points out that even she was once a baby girl, Kevin begins to feel big-brother pride in his precious sister.

I'd Rather Have an Iguana

by Heidi Stetson Mario
(Talewinds, 1999)

Puzzled over all the attention focused on her baby brother, a young girl decides that she'd rather have an iguana. That is, until she secretly peeks in on the baby, and he wins her heart!

Friendship Trees (Social Studies)

Ask children to examine the picture of the characters in the treehouse. Which of Lilly's friends are present? Does the illustration support students' predictions regarding Victor from *Chester's Way*? (See Tip, page 42.) After talking about the picture, invite children to paint friendship trees on large sheets of paper. When the paint dries, have children cut several three-sided flaps on their trees and then back the flap openings with drawings of friends. Encourage children to share their trees with each of the friends represented on them.

Now I can

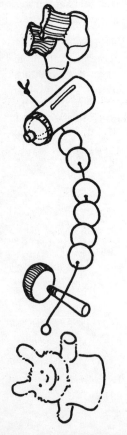

In my baby days, grown-ups helped me

Teaching With Favorite Kevin Henkes Books   Scholastic Professional Books

Lilly's Purple Plastic Purse

(GREENWILLOW BOOKS, 1996)

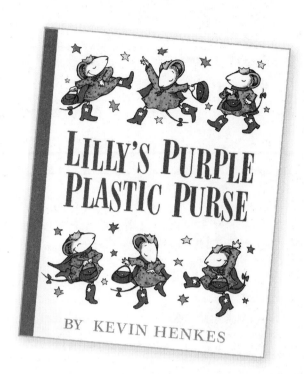

Lilly loves school and her "Wow-some" teacher, Mr. Slinger. Her feelings change, though, when he corrects her for interrupting class—and takes her new purple plastic purse! In response, the headstrong Lilly slips an angry note into her teacher's bag. But her anger dissolves into regret when she discovers the kind gestures that Mr. Slinger tucked into her purse before returning it to her. What can she do to express her remorse? With support from her understanding parents, Lilly works out a solution, and the respect and admiration between student and teacher is quickly restored.

Lilly experienced a wide range of emotions in this story. Help children list her many emotions on chart paper. Then review the story to find events that caused Lilly to experience each emotion on the list. After discussing her many moods, invite children to join Lilly on her emotional journey. To do this, read the story once again. As you read, ask children to show facial expressions and other gestures to indicate Lilly's different emotions and moods throughout the story.

Messages and Themes

▲▲▲▲▲

◆ Everyone, including each student and teacher, is unique and special.

◆ Appropriate expressions of feelings can help avoid misunderstanding and conflict.

◆ At school, sharing enthusiasm for prized possessions is fine—at the right time!

Explore Emotions

Discuss how Lilly's feelings about Mr. Slinger changed in the story. Ask children to share about times in which they experienced temporary feeling changes toward a respected adult. Why did their feelings change? What happened to help their feelings of respect for the adult return? Encourage children to talk about the different feelings that Mr. Slinger might have experienced in the story. Explain that both students and teachers can say and do things to affect each other's feelings.

Tip

▲▲▲▲▲

Challenge children to find Chester, Wilson, and Victor in the book. How can they identify each of these characters?

Extend the Book

Advice for Lilly (Language Arts/Social Studies)

When Lilly became impatient about showing off her purse, her classmates predicted that she was heading for trouble—and they were right! Have children cut out purple copies of the purse pattern on page 55. Then have them imagine that they are Lilly's classmates. On their purple purses, ask students to write their advice to Lilly about her decision to interrupt the class. Then instruct them to fold their purses where indicated, with the flap overlapping the top. If desired, invite children to decorate the outside of their purses. To use, pretend to be Lilly during group time. Open the purses one at a time to read each student's advice.

Excellent Choice! (Language Arts)

Any activity below is an excellent choice to reinforce language arts with your children!

◎ Make a checklist of some of the classroom items pictured in the book. Send small groups of students on a scavenger hunt to find similar items in your classroom.

◎ Look at the "Mice" word family on Mr. Slinger's chalkboard. Challenge children to create other word families and then make up rhymes using their listed words.

◎ Ask children to write and illustrate stories titled "Wow! What a Teacher!" Their stories might be based on real or imaginary teachers.

◎ Have students compare Mr. Slinger's classroom to their own. Invite them to design, draw, and describe the perfect classroom and its most interesting features.

◎ Invite children to create a star-covered bulletin board titled "Wow!" on which to display their works of writing.

School Is Cool!

(Language Arts)

Lilly loved lots of different things about her school experience. Give children 4- by 18-inch strips of white construction paper. Have them evenly divide their strips into three sections. Then ask them to use crayons to write or draw something that they love about school in each section. Have them paint a light red watercolor wash over their drawings so that the strips resemble rows of bricks. On a bulletin board, construct a school building using the bricks. Add details such as doors, windows, and the school name. Then title the display "School Is Cool!"

In the News (Social Studies)

Lilly and Mr. Slinger each viewed the "purse" incident from different perspectives. Invite children to conduct simple news interviews to explore the different views of the two characters. To begin, enlist volunteers to design poster bodies of both characters. Then invite student pairs to assume the roles of Lilly and Mr. Slinger by holding the corresponding posters in front of them. Then ask student reporters to interview both characters with toy microphones to broadcast their sides of the story. Afterward, ask the audience to share their opinions about the situation.

Career of the Day (Social Studies/Math)

Lilly had lots of career ideas for her future. Ask children to write their career preferences on sticky notes. Then use the notes to create a career graph. Determine from the graph results which career preference is most popular among your students. Then invite children to share their career dreams with the class. Periodically repeat this activity throughout the year to see how students' career aspirations change.

Explore Emotions

Review and compare the two events in the story that caused Lilly's stomach to lurch and made her feel like crying. Ask children to tell about experiences that might cause them to have similar feelings.

Tip

Lilly loved to hear her boots go clickety-clickety-click. Invite children to tap out rhythm patterns with a pair of boots. Can their classmates clap out the same rhythm patterns?

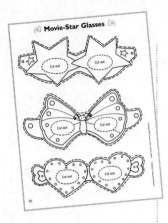

Movie-Star Glasses
(Art/Language Arts)

Lilly's new movie-star glasses featured diamonds and a chain like Mr. Slinger's. Invite children to create their own fancy glasses. Give each child a copy of page 56. Have children select and cut out a pair of glasses, and decorate them with craft jewels, glitter, and sparkly stickers. Help children attach pipe-cleaner ear pieces to their glasses and, if desired, a yarn chain. Children will enjoy using the glasses to retell or act out parts of the story.

Movin' to the Music   (Movement/Music)

Remind children that Lilly and Mr. Slinger perform an interpretive dance in the story. Then invite them to sport their movie-star glasses (see activity, above) and perform interpretive dances to assorted musical selections.

I'm Growing, I'm Learning
(Language Arts/Social Studies)

Children will have fun following Lilly's life as she appears in each of three books: *Chester's Way*, *Julius, the Baby of the World*, and *Lilly's Purple Plastic Purse*. Invite children to discuss ways in which Lilly changes in the books. Then make these boot-shaped mini-books to help children examine ways in which they, like Lilly, have changed.

◎ Give children multiple copies of the boot pattern on page 57.

◎ Ask children to write their names on the stars, then title one boot "I'm Growing, I'm Learning,"

◎ Invite children to draw pictures of or write about their accomplishments on additional boots.

◎ Staple the tops of the boots together to create booklets to share.

Book Links

My Teacher's My Friend
P. K. Hallinan
(Ideals Children's Books, 1989)

From the start of each school day right to the very end, there are many different ways that a teacher is a friend. Rhyming text and colorful illustrations feature a teacher and her class engaged in a variety of fun activities.

Show and Tell Day
by Anne Rockwell
(HarperCollins, 1997)

Ten students share their special items and personal stories on the best day of the week—Show and Tell Day! This story perfectly exemplifies how important it is to children to be able to share about themselves with others.

Dear Lilly,

_____

_____

_____

_____

_____

_____

_____

_____

_____

From, _____

Movie-Star Glasses

Cut out.

Cut out.

Cut out.

Cut out.

Cut out.

Cut out.

Teaching With Favorite Kevin Henkes Books   Scholastic Professional Books

I'm Growing, I'm Learning

Wemberly Worried

(GREENWILLOW BOOKS, 2000)

Messages and Themes

▲▲▲▲▲▲

◆ Different children worry about different things.

◆ Adults can help ease a child's anxieties.

◆ Worry does not improve or resolve a situation.

Day and night, Wemberly worries about big, small, and in-between things. She even worries about Petal, her favorite toy bunny. As the first day of school approaches, Wemberly adopts an entirely new set of worries much bigger than any of her past worries. And, in spite of her parents' calm reassurances, she carries her worries to school with her on the first day. Then Wemberly meets Jewel and Nibblet. Before long, her busy day is over—and so are most of her worries!

Discuss the alliterative title of this book. Ask children to name the other Kevin Henkes story with an alliterative title. (*Lilly's Purple Plastic Purse*)

Challenge children to find Lilly in the Halloween parade. What clues helped them identify her?

Wemberly and Jewel used their stuffed toys as a source of security and a means by which to express their worries and fears. Invite children to select and use stuffed animals to talk out their worries.

What Worries Wemberly? (Language Arts)

Wemberly worried about things at home, at the playground, and about school. Title a three-column chart "What Worries Wemberly?" and label the columns with these locations. Ask children to list things that worry Wemberly at or about each place. Do any of your students have similar worries?

Explore Emotions (Social Studies)

What makes children worry? Why? What helps to ease their worries? Do any of them have worry objects, such as stuffed bunnies? After your discussion, display a stuffed bunny with an empty facial tissue box. Invite children to write their worries on note cards and insert them in the box. Later, review the worry cards one at time. Then discuss things that might help ease the worriers' concerns.

Dear Wemberly (Language Arts)

Have children choose from the worries listed on the class-generated chart (see What Worries Wemberly?, above). Ask them to write letters to Wemberly to help ease her worries about the items that they selected. Encourage them to include their own solutions and positive outcomes to similar worries.

Book Links

I Don't Want to Go Back to School
by Marisabina Russo
(Greenwillow, 1994)

Older sister Hannah teases Ben about his "what if" anxieties over the new school year. But the first day brings relief to Ben's worries—and a comical twist to Hannah's experience!

It's Time for School, Stinky Face
by Lisa McCourt
(Bridgewater Books, 2000)

A mother creatively reassures her anxious son as he imagines a variety of unusual and unlikely school situations.

100th Day Worries
by Margery Cuyler
(Simon & Schuster, 2000)

Worry-warrior Jessica grows more and more anxious over her 100th day assignment. Finally, inspired by her family, Jessica overcomes the worry barrier to complete her assignment in a most unique way.

Activities for Teaching With More Kevin Henkes Books

Explore additional books by Kevin Henkes with the following ideas.

Bailey Goes Camping

(GREENWILLOW BOOKS, 1985)

When his older brother and sister set out on a camping trip, young Bailey feels unfairly left behind. In spite of their efforts, Bailey's parents cannot distract him from his gloom. Then Mama devises a spirit-lifting plan that allows Bailey to experience all the thrills of camping—right at home!

The Present and Future

Use this idea to help children understand that, like Bailey, they are just too young to do some things. To begin, label a two-column chart with "When I'm older, I can…" and "But for now, I can…." Brainstorm with children some things that they may not be able do now but will be able to do in the future, such as write in cursive, drive a car, or camp with the scouts. List their responses in the first column. Explain that as they grow and learn, they'll develop the skills, size, and strength to do some of the things listed. Discuss children's ideas about things they can do now to prepare for activities they'd like to try in the future. Write their responses in the second column and then try some of the preparation activities together.

Under the Starry Sky

To conclude his camping experience, Bailey fell asleep under the stars. Have children close their eyes and imagine that they are camping under the big, starry sky. (If desired, play soft music or a recording of nighttime nature sounds for inspiration.) What images run through students' minds as they enjoy the peaceful night? After a short period of time, have children create colored chalk drawings of their imaginings on dark construction paper. Display the pictures on a night scene background.

Jessica

(GREENWILLOW BOOKS, 1989)

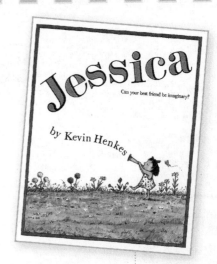

Ruthie didn't have a dog, a cat, or a brother or sister. But she had the next best thing—her imaginary friend, Jessica. Like all best friends, the two were inseparable. So, naturally, Jessica is right there with Ruthie on the first day of school. But while Ruthie is attending to her imaginary friend, she nearly misses the chance for something even better—meeting a real Jessica!

Jessica Speaks Out

Find the page on which the teacher announces everyone's name. Point out that Ruthie is talking to the imaginary Jessica. She doesn't realize that the real Jessica, sitting nearby, might think that Ruthie is speaking to her. Ask children to predict what might happen if Jessica responds to Ruthie at this point in the story. Invite small groups to create and act out a new story from this event.

Two-by-Two

Ruthie's class lined up two-by-two to march to the lavatory. Have children explore grouping with this movement activity. To begin, ask students to line up two-by-two. Does everybody have a partner? How many sets of partners are there? Invite the partners to move around the room to a selection of marching music. Then have children ungroup themselves and repeat the activity, this time lining up by threes or fours!

Dear Jessica

Ask children to share their ideas about Ruthie's feelings for the imaginary Jessica at the end of the story. Does Ruthie spend time with her anymore? What might Ruthie tell her imaginary friend about her friendship with the real Jessica? Then have students imagine that they are Ruthie. Ask them to write messages to each Jessica to explain how each one is a special friend.

Good-bye, Curtis

ILLUSTRATED BY MARISABINA RUSSO
(GREENWILLOW BOOKS, 1995)

After forty-two years as a letter carrier, Curtis recalls many pleasant memories on his last round of deliveries. Along the way, he also collects an assortment of treats and well-wishes from his mail patrons. But the biggest treat of all awaits him at the last house on the last street. Surprise!

Cards of Thanks

A number of thank-you cards awaited Curtis on his last day of work. Ask children to design cards for the helpers in their school—for example, the cafeteria and playground staff. They can write expressions of appreciation inside the cards, then deliver them in person, or ask the office staff if they can place the cards in the corresponding staff mail boxes.

Delivery Relay

Curtis delivered his mail on foot. But do your students know that mail can be transported by land, sea, and air? After discussing some different delivery methods, invite children to play this mail-delivery relay game. To begin, set up two identical obstacle courses with a mailbox at the end of each one. Divide your class into teams of four students. Then have team members assign themselves the roles of letter carrier, truck driver, airplane pilot, and ship captain. To play, the letter carriers from two different teams stand near the end of the team's course. The other members stand at designated spots along the course. On a signal, each team transports a letter from member to member until it reaches the letter carrier, who then deposits it into the mailbox.

Mail Station

Stock your writing center with paper, white labels cut into stamp-size pieces, stamp-and-ink sets, assorted envelopes, and a mailbox. Let children visit the center to create their own stationery and stamps. Then have them write letters to classmates, seal the letters in labeled envelopes, and deposit the envelopes into the mailbox for a letter carrier to deliver.

Tip

▲▲▲▲▲

For an interesting challenge, have children perform different actions such as hopping, skipping, crawling, and walking backward to deliver their mail.

More Books by Kevin Henkes

◎ ***The Biggest Boy*** Illustrated by Nancy Tafuri (Greenwillow Books, 1995)

Billy and his parents imagine that he is the biggest boy in the world. He's so big that his mother says he can blow around the clouds and toss the sun like a ball. And his father says that he will have to drink from lakes and can hang a rainbow around his neck. But in reality, Billy is just the right size for a boy his age—and so are his dreams!

◎ ***Clean Enough*** (Greenwillow Books, 1982)

Time drifts by as a young boy gets absorbed in his bath time play and adventures. Then his mother calls him out of the tub. But he hasn't even begun to wash himself! Well, surely he's clean enough…after all, he has been in the tub a long time.

◎ ***Circle Dogs*** Illustrated by Dan Yaccarino (Greenwillow Books, 1998)

The circle dogs stretch out of their sleep and start the day with good-morning kisses for everyone. Throughout the day, they run and dig. They smell Baby's face and lick Big Sister. They eat, sleep, and dream. Then they romp, jump, and bounce around some more. At day's end, the busy circle dogs once again curl up for the night.

◎ ***Grandpa and Bo*** (Greenwillow Books, 1986)

Grandpa and Bo spend their summer together walking, telling stories, laughing, and learning from each other. Then the summer draws to an end, and it's time for Bo to leave—but not before the two spot and wish upon the same shooting star! And their wishes? Well, that's a secret, but there's no doubt that the two are exactly the same.

◎ ***Oh!*** Illustrated by Laura Dronzek (Greenwillow Books, 1999)

When the snow falls at night, the morning is covered with white—and everyone wants to play! After a full day of play, the sky turns dark and it's time to rush home. Then the snow begins to fall again. Oh!

◎ ***Shhhh*** (Greenwillow Books, 1989)

A young girl is first to rise on a quiet, sleepy morning. She silently moves around the house as her stuffed animals, the dog, the cat, the baby, and her parents sleep peacefully. Shhhh. She doesn't want to wake them. Not yet, anyway. Then, with a surprise good-morning greeting, everyone springs from sleep to start the new day!

Tip

▲▲▲▲▲

Look for these out-of-print books in your local media center:

◆ ***Once Around the Block***
Illustrated by Victoria Chess (Greenwillow Books, 1987)

◆ ***All Alone***
(Greenwillow Books, 1981)

◆ ***Margaret Taylor***
(Greenwillow Books, 1983)

Author Study Celebration

Conclude your Kevin Henkes author study with these activities. Then hold a Kevin Henkes fair to celebrate the books of this well-loved author.

◎ Poll children to determine which book is the overall class favorite. Display a selection of Kevin Henkes books on a table. To vote, ask children to label sticky notes with their names. Then have them affix their sticky notes to the cover of their favorite book. Count the names on each book to discover the winning title.

◎ Display the class favorite in a place of honor along with a recording of the story.

◎ Display and review all of the story charts. (See page 8.) Encourage children to compare the stories, discussing any recurring themes or characters, unresolved issues, or issues that might arise in the future.

◎ Invite children to dress up as their favorite Kevin Henkes characters. Ask them to model their outfits and to tell about events experienced by their characters. Be sure to take photos of your "live" characters to add to your Kevin Henkes's memorable character photo album or display. (See Photo Albums, page 10.)

Let's Go to the Fair!

Invite children to use the art in Kevin Henkes's books as inspiration for creating invitations to a class fair. Send the invitations home, then plan for some of the following activities for the day of the fair:

◎ Have children make a "Welcome to Our Kevin Henkes Fair" banner to display. Encourage them to decorate the banner with book titles, character pictures, and related art.

◎ Display the class's favorite book with a blue ribbon. If desired, also display the second and third place books with appropriate ribbons.

◎ Have children wear and parade their character costumes.

◎ Plan for some of your costumed students to act out story events.

◎ Display student work, projects, and booklets around the classroom.

◎ Stock a listening center with several books and the corresponding recordings.

◎ Prepare and serve foods mentioned in some of the stories—for example, crunchy cheese snacks (*Lilly's Purple Plastic Purse*), chocolate cake (*Chrysanthemum*), and peanut-butter sandwiches cut diagonally and with cookie cutters (*Chester's Way*).

Tip
▲ ▲ ▲ ▲ ▲

Check for food allergies when planning and serving snacks.